POEMS OF A LOST CHILDHOOD
Tanya Southey

Copyright © Tanya Southey 2025

All rights reserved. The author asserts her moral rights in this work through the world without waiver. No part of this book may be reproduced, or stored in a retrieval system, or transmitted in any form or by any means, electronic, mechanical, photocopying, recording or otherwise without express written permission of the publisher.

ISBN: Paperback: 978-1-925842-49-4

Internal design by Viewpoint Studio
Cover design by Kirsten Stapelberg
Illustrations by Jess Southey

Poems of a Lost Childhood

Tanya Southey

For my mother – your smile still lights the way

The author acknowledges and honours that this book was published on the land of the First Nations of Australia.

We pay our respects to their Elders past and present.

CONTENTS

POET'S NOTE	8	LEAVING	52
		REGRETS	53
CHILDHOOD LONGINGS	10	MOTHER LOVE	54
TEA FOR TWO	11	CALLING	56
CHESS	12	NEW YORK	58
OPA	14	HORNETS	59
LIBRARY BUS	15	MOMMY	60
NOT ENOUGH	16	ESKIMOS	61
MY SISTER	17	FITTING IN	62
THE POST OFFICE	18	BOOTS	64
PICNICS AT KAREE KLOOF	19	DISOBEDIENCE	65
MURRAY PARK	20	IN-BETWEEN MEETINGS	66
THE PARK	21	ST MARY'S	67
THE VLEI	22	PIGEON TOED	68
NAMES	23	GOD'S PREFERRED PRONOUN	69
FOUNTAINS OF LONGING	24	CALL ME WHEN YOU LAND	70
GERANIUMS VS MARIGOLDS	26	INHERITED TRAUMA	71
NINETEEN	27	VOWS	72
JACKIE	28	ILLUSIONS	74
WENDY	30	I CALL BACK MY POWER	75
CUPBOARDS	31	HOT DOGS	76
BOGEYMEN	32	45	78
WHAT IF?	34	ITALIAN	79
THE OUTBUILDINGS	35	KNOW ME	80
BOXES	36	TIME	81
PRINCESS	38	30 000 FT	82
LUNCHBOX	40	UNKNOWN	83
THE POPE	41	AUTUMN	84
PHYSICAL TRAINING (PT)	42		
REALITY AND FAIRIES	44	**WIND SPIRIT**	88
THE FAMILY'S CURRICULUM	46	POEMS	89
FIFTEEN FOREVER	48	KOOKABURRA	90
		LEECH	91
THE CLARITY OF ADULTHOOD	50	ABDITORY	92
GUNS	51	WIND SPIRIT	93

POET'S NOTE

When I was a partner in a consulting firm some years ago, I bumped into a colleague in a bookshop over lunch, where he was buying a business book. 'You won't believe where I found Tanya today,' he announced back at the office. 'It was in the bookstore, in a section that starts with 'P'. 'Not Politics, not Psychology...' No-one could guess. 'In the POETRY section,' he teased. I blushed. He may as well have said pornography.

In corporations I was trained to think with clinical certainty and shun emotion which added no value to the bottom line. Back then, I was a shapeshifter. I knew how to fit in, and so I mastered the language of high performance, return on investment, pivoting, and giving people a 'heads up' on risks to be managed, which amounted to anything that detracted from profit. I became a stealth poet, a part-time feeler, an imposter of the balance sheet.

But I have always written poetry as an antidote to living in world that values 'doing' over 'being'. When I write, I lose and find myself. I lose the harsh edges of delivery in a world of gendered and other inequalities. I find the self I really am. I lose the need to be a good daughter, mother, sainted other. I find a voice, that is unfamiliar and familiar all at once. Crisp, nuggets of words suddenly coalesce before me, channelled from a self I left behind in my efforts to save anyone who needed saving.

I have written since I was six, wild expansive stories of horses kidnapped by communists, to which my teacher responded, 'What rubbish!' with a red Bic pen. So, I went underground and delivered the cliches the education system expected. At home I could be anything, as long as it involved being a Catholic. I wrote anguished poems of teenage love and spiritual poems of life and family which I unveiled to a tiny audience. In my twenties, I fantasised about writing and read anything with words between a cover. I vowed to finish reading any book I started, even if it was terrible.

In my thirties I picked up my pen again, to capture the death of my beloved grandmother, and relive the injustices of South Africa, the country in which I grew up.

I love poetry for the lilt, the swing, the sudden unexpected turns, the photographs of words which take a snapshot of humanity. Poems can describe the world, a story, a memory in just a few lines. This offering Poems of a Lost Childhood is a retrieval of myself. It is an acknowledgement that I was born into a chaotic but loving family, in a town and country that hid under a veil of conservatism and my own spirit that did not want a bar of it.

This collection is divided into two sections, memories of my childhood and reflections on my childhood as an adult. I hope it sparks your memories and helps you reconnect with your inner child, the one who still sometimes so desperately needs a play, a hug or a bit of rest.

Tanya Southey
Melbourne, 2025

CHILDHOOD LONGINGS

TEA FOR TWO

I had a porcelain tea set –
white, with painted roses,
red surrounded
by deep green leaves

It came in a box
with a clear see-through pane
and moulded plastic
that held the teapot
and its small plates
and cups snugly

The box held as much joy
as the set itself and
fitting it all back into
its rightful place was
a bonus puzzle

My father loved its elegance
we would sing
'Tea for two and two for tea,
me for you and you for me'

When he was at work
I would nest
under the floribunda tree,
bricks gathered from a pile
in the garden –
a plank of wood
for my table

My trusty teddy
poised to eat the red berries
picked from the thick hedge
between us and the neighbours

I was certain
even in the uncertainty
that tea in a china cup
could save you from anything.

CHESS

On Wednesday nights
my father loved
to play chess
with his friends
smoking and speaking
of who knows what

But I'd fling my three-year old
body to the ground
and cling to his legs
like a sobbing vine
when he said he was going

'Going'
was not a word I liked

It was lonely
scary,
his large frame buckled under
the puny weight of my body

He stayed and instead
taught me the game,
but not to smoke,
and I learnt of bishops
who moved diagonally
queens who
needed protection
and pawns who could
be sacrificed for a higher purpose.
'You'll drive her mad'
my gran proclaimed,
'She's too young for chess.'
'She's smart,' said my dad
'She knows what she's doing.'

I take both of those as beliefs
into adulthood

Years later
I go much further than
my parents ever wanted me to

From Australia I try to get my dad out,
get him going, get him connected
to interests outside of home
but he shrugs and sighs
'I gave up chess and choir for you.'

Checkmate.

OPA

His blue eyes say
we need to sit still
hold the knife,
hold the fork,
hold the feeling,
swallow it down

It's not hard to eat
the vegetable soup,
with celery and parsley

'Celery salt,' says my gran
'is the secret ingredient of love.'

As are the blessed pancakes
covered in the joy
of cinnamon and sugar

But first my aunt and I prance,
with our can-can knees and flailing arms
dancing round and round the table, singing
'Crazy horse in Paris France. Crazy.'

LIBRARY BUS

I need to get there early
be first in the queue
as the Library Bus turns the corner
and stops against the kerb

I must not be on the swings
the slide is too slippery
for the mission
I must anticipate the spot
where it will come to rest
and please let it not be beside the gaggle
of mothers gossiping in the sun
with mine nowhere to be seen

She doesn't read

The two Afrikaans sisters –
one who drives the bus
muscled armed and permed hair
will open the door,
the other similarly cloned
will hold the stamp that gives you
temporary custody of a world
between two covers

Three steep winding steps
will take me to two shelves
of children's stories

Here I will find my escape

Adventure in my hands
words weaving
me into fantasy

I will carry my prize home
and burrow from the chaos
in the structure of the story
neatly put together
while everything in the house
swirls in a vortex.

NOT ENOUGH

'Bless me Father for I have sinned,'
I say by rote
after weeks of Sr Felicity's ruler
poised above us
to stamp out any mistakes

The velvet curtain,
the kneeling bench,
hard
no cushions

'Cushions are for Protestants'
my grandparents say,
the priest shadowed
behind the grill

The tiny space is just enough
for one adult to kneel,
the smell of wood polish
mingling with my transgressions

Even at six I know
I need to be more
to ever be enough.

MY SISTER

My mother's belly swells
with the possibility
of someone else with whom to share
my fear and secrets

Everyone tells me
'You're going to be a big sister'
'You must help your mommy;'
'She's going to be tired;'

I first see her close up
as my mother carries
her into the car
and cradles her
as I lean between
the black vinyl seats
of the red Valiant

My father drives us home
seat-beltless,
careening untethered
through the world.

THE POST OFFICE

The Post Office
is a place of sorting

Not just letters

The red polished
concrete floors
the brass bars
behind which
they weigh your envelope
on a miniature scale
to determine how many
stamps you need

There are two doors
on either side
of the dividing walls
that sort us

Whites/Blankes and
Non-whites/Nie Blankes

You may not go through the door
not meant for you

At eight, I stand at the counter
and strain my head against the bars
to try and see what's on the other side.

PICNICS AT KAREE KLOOF

An hour's drive
through mielie fields
past a lonesome general store
with Coke signs
tyres
hay bales
fresh vegetables
oil changes advertised
next to coveted ice cream logos

With Dutch songs, hymns
sung in rounds
sweaty legs
sticking to vinyl car seats

The smell of polony sandwiches
and the prospect of chocolate sprinkles
on thickly buttered bread,
tea tasting of thermos flask
in plastic picnic cups

An hour's drive to be released
into the wild,
climb trees in dense canopy,
jump over gurgling streams,
lichened rocks,
a 'wag-n-bietjie' bush
catching the back
of your jumper,
suspending you as you
listen to the
Sakkabulla bird calling

An hour's drive
from anxiety
to freedom.

MURRAY PARK

We weren't allowed to go
to Murray Park on weekends -
too many people drinking beer -
Afrikaans men with fast fists
and short tempers

Who knew what could happen
to English-speaking Catholics?

Instead, my grandfather
took us on Thursday afternoons,
a lone camper may be there,
the 'boys' – grown men in khaki,
mowing the lawn
while their white supervisor
watched, bored and smoking

We spread our blanket
close to the swings,
running, to burn off our energy,
hoping we'd be there long enough
to see the horses
galloping, wild from the paddocks
to be tamed in the barn for the night.

THE PARK

'We're going to the park,' I'd yell

Over the road from our house,
in the suburb my grandfather
had architected,
where the sentry
of pine trees he'd planned
made our street an 'avenue'

The clay soil squelched
between our toes,
black, with a swampy smell

We squealed and threw our darkened feet
to the heavens as we pushed ourselves
higher and higher
beyond the limits of the swings,
singing Abba,
careful not to graze our bare toes
on the tar beneath us

Factions formed fast
in small parochial towns

When the Afrikaans kids arrived
we'd break into warring tribes,
dig clay from the hole
near the rocking boat
roll it into little balls
and throw them at each other
from the end of willow sticks

Evidence of our valour
still under our nails
at bath time.

THE VLEI

The park had a small bridge
built to cross the vlei

Full of reedy water
from the Blesbokspruit,
we were told
not to enter it,
never to drink it
for fear of
'bilharzia'
a tiny snail
choosing to set up home
in your kidneys

Being sick was forbidden,
too many Hail Mary's and prayers
to the Saint of Hopeless Cases
followed by the
'How dare you make us worry?'
when you'd recovered

So, we tentatively made our way
down the embankment
to stand on the rocks
to avoid the water
while the Afrikaans kids
swam and splashed
as if nothing could touch them.

NAMES

In a small town
everyone has a name
except him

My mother names him
'Blue Truck,'
but 'Red Face'
'Slicked Hair' or 'Cold Eyes'
would have equally done the job,
however, 'Blue Truck' sticks.

He suddenly appears
while we're walking home,
driving slowly next to us
asking when he can come visit
and do we need a ride?

'If he asks, your name is Susan.
Don't give him your real name.'
Mum whispers

I am not used to her resolve,
her pretence of a life we do not live

We stop and talk to a woman tending
her roses, and mum says
'He's following us.'

'Come in,' she says
and we drink her orange juice
while Blue Truck circles the block

In her seventies my mum and I
are sipping tea

'My name is Susan,' I say with a wry grin—
her eyes grow wide,
'Blue Truck,' she responds
speaking both of fear
and the relief that we got away.

FOUNTAINS OF LONGING

It could be any Saturday,
I hold my father's
big, calloused hands
as we walk through the streets
from banks to bakeries

The fountains
peppered around our town
with their blue mosaic tiles
invite us to paddle
even though it's not allowed

The water shoots up
and collapses in the rhythm
of the heartbeat of our dreams

Stopping at the water's edge
to observe the coins
of others' wishes
shining up in hope

I lean on the wall

'Can I have a coin dad, to make a wish?'

'You don't wish with my money,' he says

He sees the hobo
on the ground,
his hand bleeding,
a broken beer bottle beside him

In the chemist
dad buys a bandage and antiseptic
and returns to wrap his hand

A toothless, alcoholic grin,
a weathered sunburnt face

Some wishes
are for kindness
but my childish heart
just wanted to throw a carefree coin
amongst all the others.

GERANIUMS VS MARIGOLDS

My grandmother prunes
her geraniums
never a dead leaf
nor withered branch

They flower
consistently
symmetrical
in neat lined up boxes
perfectly equidistant
in between the windows

At home we plant
the marigold seeds
in our flowerless garden
and watch them grow
wildly into the lawn.

NINETEEN

'How old will you be when you die?'
Kim asks,
we are only twelve
yet my body recoils

I have a deep knowing
that to put a number to it
is to dance on a tightrope
with a fateful demon

'I won't say.'

'You must,' she insists
with pressure that warns
of friendship breaking

'You go first.'

'Nineteen,' she says

'That's young, it won't happen.'
'I'll be old, really old, forty-six,'
I comply

Kim is nineteen and nine months
when she dies

I turn forty-six and wait
hypervigilant
for my young folly
to be revealed

Yet the year passes,
and my prophetic ability
is laid to rest
as I blow out the candles
on my next birthday.

JACKIE

'Can Jackie sleep over?'

It is an innocent question
a plea for fun,
friends, midnight giggles

'Your mother will go to jail,'
Kim tells me after the weekend

The school bus
drops me on the main road
I run home panicked,
the brown winter grass
crunching beneath my fearful feet

Will they have already taken her away?

The front door stands ajar
the kitchen is empty
the kettle silent
a knife with butter and jam
lies on the table
the house is a mess

Raided already?
It's hard to tell

I call her name.

No reply

Will they take my father too?

I am stricken in the kitchen

Then
through the window
I see her at the washing line
taking down the bone dry
white sheets
my black friend
slept in.

WENDY

I put salt on her pancakes
instead of sugar

I say 'Hello, hello?'
when she calls,
pretending I can't hear
then put down the phone

I leave it off the hook
so that she gets a constant
engaged signal

I do not want her to like me
the way she loves my mother,
smothering her with subterfuge

She tells me,
'You'll drive your mother
to a mental home.'
'You're bad.'

I block out her curses
as best a twelve-year-old can

'I will help your mother leave your father -
You're just like him.'

I am in control
until my mother realises
and returns the phone to its cradle.

CUPBOARDS

My gran had a built-in cupboard
in her bedroom
with solid white doors
and rigid organisation,
the key was never missing
and always in the lock

Everything arranged
in categories, colours
cooking overalls
everyday wear
church clothes
that smelled of ironing
and 'Blue Grass' her signature perfume

My sister and I loved the far-left side
the things that were not worn often,
we were instructed to be gentle with,
the thick fur coat from another time,
stroking it as if it was a dearly beloved pet

But it was the fox stole
we desired the most

The head, with a clasp
attached to the jaw
that clipped over your shoulders
while the tail hung elegantly on your arm

When we twirled, we were
transported to the young woman
my grandmother was
as she waltzed on another
continent – content, vibrant,
carefree in a long dress
protected by the fox
with his all-seeing glass beady eyes.

BOGEYMEN

There will be no television –
the government is adamant
it will ruin Christian families,
but it is not the only reason
they keep us from watching

All we have is the scratchy sound
of curated radio programs
that filter out the truth
of where and how we live

We gather round and listen
while the anthracite heater
filled with black coal
and orange flames
warms the lounge
but leaves our bedrooms freezing

The coal is delivered
to the concrete bunker
at the back of our house -
a little 'house'
with a hole in the 'roof'

In summer when it is empty
we dare each other
to climb on top
and lower ourselves
into the windowless world
where monsters,
spiders or snakes might live

We crawl filthy from the chute
squealing at our bravery

But in winter the delivery men
with hessian over their backs
and necks, pile off the truck
with the sacks of coal
on their shoulders, yelling
'Woza, woza,' at each other
as they run into the garden
in packs, filling the coal bunker
while my mother pays
the white driver and
we stand in the biting highveld cold
unaware that the coals
of justice will soon be lit.

WHAT IF?

What if you die?
What if you get kidnapped?
What if I never see you again?
What if you miss the bus home?

All families have questions

In ours they were calamities
with the same severity

On a Sunday afternoon
my father would sit
working hard on the
Tribune's crossword puzzle

He would ask the Greek café owner
to keep a paper for him
and we would buy it at lunch time
after mass and tea with my grandparents
so that he had a chance to win R20 000
– a small fortune in those days

And on those afternoons,
as the pigeons coo-ed
and the crickets started chirping
and the sun floated on dust motes
through the dining room window
we tried a different question:

What if we won a lot of money?

As we dreamed of a life that wasn't ours.

THE OUTBUILDINGS

Every house had
a tiny outside room with a toilet –
maybe a shower and basin

Our 'toilet' was a concrete
hole in the ground
over which the porcelain lavatory
could have easily been placed,
but why would you go to such expense
when the room was made for servants?

I feared that tiny dark room,
Jeyes Fluid smells,
dank water,
the strange
chain that hung above the hole
allowing you to flush to who knows where?

We never had servants
definitely not ones who lived
on our property
so, the room
became a place for discarded dreams,
canvasses my father half-painted,
broken furniture,
lawn mower parts,
lamps that failed to shine

Artefacts of who he could have been
if he was able to live his Dante-filled dreams
and paint like Michelangelo.

BOXES

There were three boxes
in my grandmother's house
that held my attention
for hours

The box of loose buttons
in the 'kleine kamertje' -
the 'little lounge'
that housed the piano,
games in the cupboard,
sewing supplies

This old brown chocolate tin
held buttons in the shape of flowers,
leather buttons, crystals, buttons
with two holes, four holes,
or just a little loop at the back

We would line them up,
sort them into favourites,
wondering what their stories were
and where they came from

In the lounge
on the coffee table,
stood the heavy brass box,
scenes from ancient Rome
on the lid and the sides,
a small brass latch
needed to be lifted
to find what was inside

A ball of string,
a cork with 'Wedding Anniversary 1978'
written in my grandfather's
architectural print
elastic bands, stamps, and postcards
that needed a reply

But the box I loved the most
was on my grandmother's dressing table -
her jewellery box -
with treasures of a lifetime
broaches
bangles
earrings and her trademark
tiger's eye pieces
I wondered if they really
belonged to tigers,
never quite sure if I liked them

But the one I always ran my fingers over
was the red stone necklace
they said turned white
just before someone died,
my gran vowed she'd never wear it,
this ominous heavy necklace
that foretold the future.

PRINCESS

I turn old frogs
into willing servants
as I grow into myself
and jester my way
through the dreamless
landscape of our town,
and so
my grandfather falls
under my spell

Perhaps it's my golden hair
the copy/paste DNA
I share with his daughters,
or maybe he's mellowing

The rules at my grandparent's house
lull me into safety:

"Dry between your toes
to avoid rheumatism,'
'Put on slippers
as soon as you are out of the bath,
not a speck of dirt
should be taken into bed,'
'No splashing on the floor,'
'And don't even think about not loving
our dogs.'

My grandfather had a note in his wallet
'In case of an accident
I am Catholic – call a priest;
and please find my dogs
at 84th Fifth Street and
take them to my daughter
at 22 Hagart Avenue.'

I knew exactly how to fit in,
tick off the checklist,
get the gold stars,
until my teenage rebellion set in

But when I was nine
my grandfather Frans
would bring me tea
with two Marie biscuits
in his dressing gown
kneeling on his slippers

He would shuffle in
like a tiny jester
in a fairy-tale,
'Princess,' he would say,
'James at your service.'

LUNCHBOX

Lisa had a bento box
before a bento box
was even in my vernacular

A stylish orange Tupperware
with 70's flair,
small compartments
that held a cornucopia of treats -
biltong sandwiches,
carefully cut fruit,
a tiny Belgian chocolate

My wax wrapped
white bread
was cut by hand,
thick, uneven slices
held together
with too much
butter
peanut butter and
crystallised syrup

I wanted to be stylish
symmetrical
just like the other kids

Love did not come
in the shape
of my longing.

THE POPE

Sister Natalie is powerful,
a woman of gravitas,
she can see straight through your
 'Dog ate my homework,' excuses

As she stands at the lectern
two hundred children fall silent
there is no need for her
to tell us to be quiet

She clears her throat
'Girls, I have sad news
the Pope is dead.'

The hush of sobriety
deepens in the hall
sending Anne and me
into giggles that make us cry

The strictest nun
with crisp blue lensed glasses
hauls us outside
Anne and I look at each other in terror

'Girls,' she pronounces
'Sometimes we laugh
at sad news,
it's called nervous laughter.'

And we nod throw our heads back
and laugh even harder.

PHYSICAL TRAINING (PT)

The blue knapsack
with the red piping
always smelled
like wet towels,
swimming costumes
and running shoes

I carried it with dread
on the days we had PT

Our six-year-old silky bodies
naked in the change rooms,
with the wooden benches
and the half blue doors

We'd giggle and stick our heads
under the doors
when we had changed
and others were still busy

We could barely dress ourselves -
let alone read our names
on the labels our mothers
stitched onto our uniforms -
as we put on our thick
black regulation bathing suits
and our bathing caps which
sorted us into
our sporting house colours

The concrete floor was wet
from all the classes
before ours

I lagged at the back
as my friends
squealed and jumped
into the water, chalky
with too much chlorine

I stood on the top step
teeth chattering
crying for my mother
who swam with joy

Mrs van Vuuren in her blue track suit
extracted my grip from the handles
and pushed me into the water
commanding us to hold the edge
put our faces under water and kick

I kicked but held my head up high
grimacing at the splashes.

She pushed my head under

I came up spluttering
wanting to live

The absence of love
feels like drowning.

REALITY AND FAIRIES

We wander through
the bushy paths,
rockeries and succulents
lining the way to playgrounds
and classrooms

Behind rocks, bluebells hide fairies,
witches live in gnarled resin
at the base of trees
and gnomes protect patches
of lichen and moss

We take in the wonder
of this other world
that lives beside our human one

The gardener digs and scrapes
keeping the fairy gardens magical,
he pulls rounds of hosepipes
across the hockey field
and the water sprays to its own
staccato rhythm from brown to green

His name is Abraham -
but we call him the 'garden boy'
and in the summer sun we are pierced
by the ray of our principal's morals -
'Abraham is a man,' we are told
and with that withering stare
we learn the vernacular of our country
is not acceptable to nuns.

Too young to fully comprehend,
later we begin to see that ogres
are not just in fairy tales -
we have all been living under a spell

We don't live in fairy land
but in a brutal place
where men are boys
just because their skin is darker
than ours.

THE FAMILY'S CURRICULUM

Homework
was a burden
on days when the sky
was as blue
as my school dress -
which was most days

It was a blessing
when my father
fear-filled, money-obsessed
flew into a rage -
which was most days

Screaming for the twenty cents
missing from his change,
my mother's folly
for buying us a lolly

Bury my nose in a book,
find the square root
of perceived poverty,
balance the equation
of unequal relationships,
find the answer to
the metal's weight
in my family's periodic table -
steel -
not a pure metal -
but heavy none the less

The boilermaker's daughter
born of the forge

Daddy's temper
crashing banging,
the heat of discontent
carried home from the factory
that drowned the opera
in his soul

'I can't do my homework,' I'd scream -
the only plea that would stop his tirade,
not the hurt he was inflicting,
not the neighbours peering over the fence,
not the threat of us all leaving him,
but the fear that his daughter would fail
and repeat the poverty cycle,
trapped in manual labour when
there was art and literature

Perhaps in this fearful harshness
there was also love.

FIFTEEN FOREVER

I remember when I met you
a thousand stars fell from the sky
and landed at my feet

Covered in stardust
I knew the holiness of seconds
where once again you existed
next to me

On this planet, in this time
when the noon day sun was angling
through the windows of ordinariness
and the wind lay on the ground
in reverence to what it witnessed

The waves of the ocean bowed
and prayed a benediction of love

And birds took flight
in rounds of joy
dipping in the wonder of it all

Souls reunited
again

Always.

THE CLARITY OF ADULTHOOD

GUNS

I push the pram,
she's tiny,
dressed in pink -
a stereotype
I was never going
to clothe her in,
but the gifts from
well wishers
coloured her with love

In the store
I announce, 'I want a gun.'

'This is a great ladies' gun,
it will fit in your handbag
and you can kill someone
from three metres,'
the salesman smiles

The black metal
is cold in my hands,
which only want to protect
the soft pink bundle

I return the gun to the counter

I cannot teach her
how broken
the world is

We go home
take out the atlas
and plan our escape.

LEAVING

'We're emigrating,' I tell people,
going to Australia
to live a different life

Those determined to remain tell us
'You'll be back.'

My anxiety for getting things wrong
is on radar alert

U-turns are not allowed
failure is not an option

Shame has haunted me
in every childhood
choice that was not mine to make

To counteract the naysayers
before I leave for a country
I have never been to
I begin to tell people
'I am going home.'
'I didn't know you were Australian,' they say

'I am not, but I am going to be,'
I mutter defiantly.

REGRETS

They had walked in just before us
refined, well dressed
ready for a night
of food, wine and connection

As a child we ate at restaurants
twice a year,
on someone's birthday,
or an anniversary,
and now at seventeen,
ushered to a small booth
I felt grown up,
pretending to be
more sophisticated
than I felt

The tall buildings of Johannesburg
rose above my small-town dreams
unfamiliar, grand, majestic

As we read our menus
the manager began whispering
to the only black couple in the restaurant
his arm pointing to the door

As the woman rose
in her beautiful clothes
she fell to the ground and said,
'Let me crawl out on my knees,
not allowed to eat in my own country.'

If I could turn back time
and lose my people-pleasing ways,
forget that I was schooled
to avoid causing a scene,
I would have crawled out with her.

MOTHER LOVE

Mum is talking to the dog
'You're. A. Gut. Boy,'
she says emphasising each word
in a fake accent reserved
for the special love
of the half Chihuahua
whose front legs are longer
than his back legs,
a specimen of spare parts
that mum thinks is pure beauty

We snicker behind her back,
and to her face too,
about her ability to love the unlikely

Mum loves the security guards
stationed at the gates of her suburb,
she breaks into loud Zulu
telling them it might rain
and asking are they well?
Now trained in her special affection
they dance when the see her car slowing
yelling, 'Gogo, Gogo'
waving her on, through the boom gates,
their legs floppy with laughter

We smile and wave shyly
while she knits the colours
of the world together

At the supermarket Mum gathers children,
the shoeless, donut-glazed nosed ones
with wiry hair still showing evidence of
last night's sleep

She speaks Afrikaans to their mothers
and makes smiling suggestions
that they should wear a vest
and aren't their feet cold
walking barefoot in winter?
They shake their heads or
shrug their shoulders saying 'Nee, Tannie,'
but leave warmer nonetheless
being told how handsome they are

We push the trolley
filling it with groceries
while she is distracted by babies
and people she's gathered from her childhood

Mum runs after the postman
to give him a sandwich,
a beggar gets the last bread,
which means Dad will roar
as he will have no lunch
to take to work tomorrow

The pigeons are fed, the birds coo,
the neighbours have drunk all the tea,
the dishes are strewn in the lounge,
ashtrays overflow with stubbed out
gossip, giving Dad more to rage about

So much love
so liberally applied
to so many
to any

I came to realise why my dad
wanted me to protect her
from the world after he'd gone.

CALLING

I was eight when
three stray homing pigeons
took residence
under the eaves
of our garage

The same year
the ginger cat with feline leukemia
chose to arrive and live
out his last three weeks with us

Broken things had a habit
of finding my mother

She would call the birds

The spongy green kikuyu grass
beneath her feet,
the canopies of trees against the walls
of the patch we called home

What went through her head
as she whistled nature to come to her
and called the mother
into our garden?

I remember the radiant joy
on her face
as they answered,
cooing,
as she scattered the food
and they landed,
trusting, close by
yet cautious
of this gratuitous outpouring
of love

She always spread a handful
further away
for the meeker ones
so the dominant banker-like pigeon
strutting with his
self-important chest out didn't take it all

Now I stand barefoot
on my lawn
on another continent
throwing seeds
of memories
onto the lawn,
calling her close

Every now and then
as I am making breakfast
a lone dove eyes me
through the window
blinking and nodding,
both of us acknowledging
the mothers we came from.

NEW YORK

'Dad, I'm going to New York.'

'Who's going with you?'

'Just me alone, for work.'

'What kind of husband let's his wife go alone?
Besides you're blonde you will get kidnapped.'

From the other side of the world
I hear my father groan and plea
repeating the reasons for me to stay home

I'm thirty-three working
for the General Electric Company
and still, he cannot believe

I can ever be safe
without him.

HORNETS

I think of it now
with my adult brain
I imagine the nuns
planning our class excursion

Not the movies, or the ice rink,
or the wild waters of the man made
ocean park with waves and slides,
but something educational

"The Sewerage Plant,"
one of them must have declared
and so it was,
we got to have a shitty experience

Vividly, I remember the smell,
some of us coughing and heaving,
but mostly all of us giggling
standing outside on the steps

Until suddenly, my friend Jenny
bolted, screaming, moving at speed
as if we were at an athletics competition

All of us stunned as her red hair flew
across lawns, past trees,
a teacher flying behind her

It was my first encounter
of how a sting could change joy
to fear and pain in a microsecond

We don't always
see the hornets
circling our happiness.

MOMMY

1976

'Mommy,' we both scream,
my sister is sobbing,
dribble sobbing,
I cry but compose myself,
I've learned that crying hinders my running

She's leaving

The wind is flapping
her green bellbottom pants
as she storms across the park
into the sunset,
going who-knows-where
but far from my father

If I can just catch her
we will be normal,
I will fix her with jokes
and music
tether her to me,
wallpaper the dysfunction,
show the world
we are just like them

2021

It's 4:30am
when the phone rings
'I am sorry, she's gone,'
the nurse says in a quiet tone.

I call my sister
bellbottoms fluttering
in my vocal cords
and utter the words
I always feared
I'd someday have to speak
'We're orphans...' I say.

ESKIMOS

Eskimos have seven different words
for snow, depending on its texture

And twenty different words for white
based on the colour against the sky

And we only have one word

For grief

And mother

How to put them in a sentence
when words have no shade?

And mother usually joyous

Has left

And taken words
and their meanings with her.

FITTING IN

I saw how they looked,
first at each other
then at us,
as we approached,
micro expressions
placing us
in the pecking order
of bake sales
and worthiness

My mother exuberant,
waving, yelling 'hello'
from an impolite distance,
her hair blowing wildly
in the wind,
her frumpy unmatched
clothes gave away
who we really were

Their sets and perms stiff,
did not yield to anything
they either waved
dismissively, entering
the church or addressed her,
hesitantly, backing away
as she leaned in

Even then, my small hand
would take hers
and drag her off to the safety
of just us, belonging
to ourselves,
unseen better than seen

But in those moments,
assigned to our pew,
I was schooled in how
I might later need to show up
to be called successful
chiselled, honed, tamed
scraped,
knowing my place

I wish I'd known
to let the suits and pearls
fall to the ground
and step into the
holiness
of being more like her.

BOOTS

I bought these boots
in Hong Kong
three days before
my dad died

Anyone looking
at them thinks
they are just light fawn
suede, zip up, pixie boots

But they knew my feet
when I still thought
the earth was solid.

The leather knows
the earth is fluid
that sinkholes
can appear
right where
you are standing.

DISOBEDIENCE

It was anarchy
to fall in love with myself
to find the gentle folds
that screamed of blindness

It was treason
to decide the earth
was my church,
birds my angels
cawing blessings
on my awakening

It was a betrayal -
to a system of oppression -
to ground myself
beneath the olive tree,
connected to the Mother,
Earth at my feet,
stars at my crown.

It was rebellion
to decide God was a woman
of substance and creation
and that loving her
was an act of defiance
in a world of warlords.

IN-BETWEEN MEETINGS

I order lunch online
and run across
to the shopping centre
to collect my salad

A tiny Nonna, holding her
daughter's hand yells
'Bella signora'
I laugh, keep walking
throwing a 'Ciao Bella'
over my shoulder with a smile

I see them again on my way back,
and she grabs me and pulls me aside
saying 'Veloce, veloce'
moving her arms
to show me my own speed

Her daughter apologises,
'Dementia,' she says
as her mother hugs
me and tells me I am beautiful

And there in the middle
of my workday
filled with
numbers, outputs
and deliverables,
standing in the thin
winter sun,
I am hugging a part
of my life -
an overexuberant mother,
an Italian father

The poetry of
family, humanity and joy
over things that will
be forgotten in time.

ST MARY'S

I was born at a dedicated maternity hospital,
designed by my architect grandfather
named after the Mother of Jesus.

I was not born at home

I was born into a world planned by grandfathers
sons of wars, the first, the second, their own
that locked them in grief, never to be expressed

I was not born at home

I was born in a sterile place
built for efficiency and disinfected calm,
reluctant to return, they used forceps to dislodge me

I was not born at home

My mother, tamed and dutiful
chiselled into submission by daily lessons
faded into an antiseptic view of who she should be

We were not born at home

Yet soil and trees
birds and sky,
wild cosmos lining highways
called us back to ourselves
and slowly we unfurled to soul nudges
that took us home
to the women we were meant to be.

PIGEON TOED

My grandmother
was pigeon toed,
she walked
right foot turned in
to greet the left

Late in her eighties
she told me
it was from kicking
the small ball
for her tiny Pomeranian

I hooted at her words
saying there was no way
a small game
turned her foot,
she disagreed:
small things
can change us deeply

So, it is with my family
changed by little dogs
and letters in the mail,
post boxes holding tight scripts
of grave news
doors closing
mirrors cracking
seismic shifts
on ladybug wings.

GOD'S PREFERRED PRONOUN

I like to speak to God
as if she is one of us
I called her 'he'
my whole childhood
and one day deep
in adulthood
when we had not
spoken for years,
I made contact
and asked her if it was okay
to speak to her again?

She laughed and said,
'Of course,
I have been listening
to you anyway
and watching you
brave it on your own.'

Relieved, I said,
'Can I call you –
She/her?'

She guffawed,
her head thrown back
and replied
'It took you so long
to finally get that right.'

CALL ME WHEN YOU LAND

Call me when you land;
give me two rings when you get home;
a missed call is fine;
send me a text when you're safe,
just the word 'home' will suffice

Let me know you get there;
that there wasn't an accident on the way;
that the plane stayed in the air;
I know 'no news is good news,'
but I need certainty,
now more than ever

Drop a feather from the sky,
send a rainbow when it's dry,
make the candle flutter,
randomly shuffle to your favourite song

Call me when you land.

INHERITED TRAUMA

I recognised that faraway look,
the one that warned 'Don't Disturb'
when Mum read the wind,
trying to decide if
it was going to rain or not

She was wired for subtle hints
of the breeze at her feet
or in her hair

She sighed
before the rage arrived
on the eastern horizon
of his anger

Now I have it too,
I can feel
that something happened
in this room, long ago
that pain sat in this chair,
that longing was planted
in the garden
next to the birch tree.

VOWS

I made my vow
on the hill of my discontent
and as I spoke it to the heavens,
I caught my echo
and reinforced it every time

I had my doubts but
reassured myself that
my ill-made promise
matched my soul

I made a vow
in the heady days of youth
repeated words
not my truth,
vows that wove
a cord to you,
vows that tethered me
with glue

I made a vow
to fit right in
to be so safe
to go within
to step inside a box
or two
to walk the path
in others' shoes

I made a vow
to shut me down
to close the channel
to my crown
to clip my wings
to ground my flight
to set aside
my ultimate birthright

I made a vow
to save them all
to turn my back
upon myself
and watch me fall

I made a vow
I break it now

I made a vow
I break it now

I place my hands
in dark wet soil
I feel the seedlings
as they coil
I take the green
I take the brown
I take what's me
I fit the crown

I hold the space
I leave the race
I smile and see
my own true face

I made the vow
I break it now

I made the vow
I break it now.

ILLUSIONS

They say you are gone
but I know you are only
out in the garden,
going for a walk,
enjoying the sun

They say you are gone
but I know you are only
just around the corner
peering at the doves
in the tall gum tree

They say you are gone
but I know you are only
floating on a cloud,
contemplating the stars.

I CALL BACK MY POWER

I call back my power from all places

I call back my power from the east
the pebble of myself left on a beach
the rock of my resolve lying amongst
the desires of others

I call back my power from all places

I call back my power from the west
the whisper of myself on the wind of your breath
the tenuous desire I had to be myself
in the sea of the others

I call back my power from all places

I call back my power from the south
the dew on the mountain glinting in the sun
the juicy early morning of a life well begun

I call back my power from all places

I call back my power from the north
the idea of my own divinity lost
in a secular world of transient whims,
the knowing that I am

I take myself back from all places

I integrate all I have loved
all that is still to be created
all that I have scattered as crumbs to the world

I call myself back from all places.

HOT DOGS

My mother never asked for anything
beyond going to church

She wore hand-me-downs
from friends
the occasional
birthday gifted clothes;
she didn't browse the racks in stores

She loved spaghetti, fish and chips,
a roast or whatever you
might cook for her

Her eyes lit up
as you set a plate in front of her,
she'd make a hasty sign of the cross
before she tucked in with gusto.

Months before she died
her appetite disappeared
not only for food but everything
except mass and prayers,
the avenues
to lead her where she was going

Sometime in that twilight,
on a sunny day,
she asked if I minded very much,
hoping it was not too much to ask,
or too much trouble
for a Vienna sausage –
she simply had to have a hot dog

All my hopes rested in this tiny meal,
perhaps her appetite was returning,
her zest for life, her energy for recovery

But all she wanted to eat was
a crispy roll, thick with butter and tomato sauce,
to let the taste linger on her lips
like childhood meals in memories.

45*

Forty-five years later
I have a conversation with your mother
I am no longer twelve and
you exist only in photographs

Your mother has carried your death
in the osteoarthritis of her regrets
set in the bones that carried you

We talk about what you might have become,
the children you might have had,
the career you could have pursued

Would you have been thin?
Would you have padded out like us?
Who would you have grown into?

We tell all the funny stories,
the antics we got up to
in the childhood bubble of joy

And later,
in our WhatsApp chat
your stoic, midwife mother
reveals how she wept
with each baby she delivered
after you were gone.

*This poem accompanies Nineteen on page 27.

ITALIAN

Madonna!
I wish I had learned to speak Italian
there are so many familiar words
in my head
that have no meaning

Sounds of my father,
his rounded vowels
an incantation
of *amore* or *brutta bestia*.

As an adult I try to
learn the sounds of his childhood,
meaning stays with me fleetingly,
the odd word remains translated,
the rest evaporate

After my father died
my cousins from Italy visited,
we spoke broken Italian,
and they, bare bone English

So instead, we passed love
between us
like a loaf of bread
and understanding like butter
as we stirred meals
added sugo to browning meat
knowing that we are family

Conversing enough
with eyes and hands and hearts
as if language
was only needed for strangers.

KNOW ME

There are so few people left
who knew me as a child
in the body I used to inhabit
my wispy blonde hair
skinny toothpick legs
fierce determination
that rose as defiance
railing to become someone others
thought I could not be.

I was a girl who wanted more
and believed she was invincible
but also obsessed about
dying and losing her family

Looking back
I survived more than I imagined
and have learnt I control nothing
and everything

And that love and connection
are more than enough
to define a life as remarkable.

TIME

If time was a spiral
and we could wait
for the moment
the memory lined up
with the now
and elegantly jump
across to then
where would you go?

So many places,
so many times,
but ordinary days
are what I would choose

My aunt in her bikini,
my mother modest
in her one-piece,
swimming cap tight
over her ears

The suburbs quiet,
except for the crickets,
a lone lawnmower
droning somewhere
and our screeches
as our tiny childhood bodies
bombed into the freezing pool
bubbles around us
as we held our noses
and came up gasping for air
triumphant in our bravery

We swam to the step,
our mothers sat with
their feet in the water,
young 'crocodiles'
our heads just above the surface
lying in wait
for the cheese and tomato sandwiches
that tasted of summer and family.

30 000 FT

I never imagined
I would write poems
at 30 000ft

Flights were for my cousins
who lived overseas,
I scratched poetry
with my blue Bic pen,
standard school issue,
in a lined exercise book.

I'd lie in the shade
my hip bones connected
to the earth
my stomach at one
with the grass
and pen poems
of wonder

My world was small
my dreams, larger
but never crossed borders

And the young girl inside me
now laughs in disbelief
at how many poems I have written
from my plane seat
as I fly through the sky
the stars above me
the earth below me
my bones filled with stories
of a life well-travelled.

UNKNOWN

You are an empty box,
blank, on the family tree
unknown to any of the living
and even my dad, long dead

You must have meant something
to someone,
certainly, to my grandmother,
even though she never
revealed your identity

She carried her shame,
wanton woman with desires
that created my father

And he in turn, ran
from his identity,
his country
and anyone who knew
of his illegitimacy

Your blank genes are
expressed in ours,
and we, unconscious,
do not know
if the curl of our lips,
the gait in our walk,
or the curve of our noses
are remnants of you.

AUTUMN

This time of year
was always only
the end of summer -
in childhood -
it meant swimming pools
and humming sunsets,
thunderstorms and gardens,
all of us eating dinner outside,
in the dwindling light

This time of year, never had the thinning
of the veil between this world and the one hereafter,
until you started slipping between here and there,
and butterflies appeared around my car
and random music shuffled on my radio
urging me to look up,
before you slipped away

This year the light is the same,
the humidity just at the tipping point,
the cool change is gathering on the horizon
and still you are gone

Summer always turns to autumn now.

This book was mainly written at Wind Spirit on sacred land looking onto Mount Wollumbin, at the foothills of the ley line that runs from the ocean in Queensland to Uluru in the red centre of the majestic country I now call home, Australia. My memories are deeply rooted in the home of my heart and my childhood, South Africa. I acknowledge all the traditional custodians who have loved the sky and soil here for over 60 000 years and my own ancestors who passed on their love, hopes and dreams in the helix of my DNA. May our collective ancestral wisdom penetrate our hearts and minds. We need that now more than ever.

I give thanks for the friendship and mentoring that Joanne Fedler has given me over the last seven years. Joanne, you have been a shepherd to my writing, a teacher of far more than the craft of writing. You have championed my work like a midwife, loving my words into existence. I bless the day our paths connected.

Kirsten Garbini, the magic we created at Wind Spirit with Joanne was the seed of this book. Thank you for the affirmation and sharing your poems with us. Kirsten Stapelberg, who gifted me her watercolour for my cover. The protea is the South African National flower and grows so well in Australia too. Your generosity and friendship are precious to me. Thank you and keep painting.

The Springs Convent Class of 1984, many of whom are mentioned in my childhood poems, you were there for it all; you are by some miracle all still in my life forty years later for which I am so grateful.

To all my family and friends, alive or behind the veil, words cannot express the joy of having you in my life. Finally, to my husband Wayne, who gives me space and cooks me meals, while I play with words, you are a gem and Jess and Lachlan who have their own special creative interests and inspire me to pursue my own. Thank you, thank you.

As an afterword, I leave you with these final poems from the writing experience at Wind Spirit.

Much love
Tanya

WIND SPIRIT

POEMS

I wake
in the middle
of the night

poems

spilling
out of me

she's hovering
above me

reminding me
not to forget

her spirit -
how gently
she cracked me
open.

Now I know
the ley line

her to me,
me to three

poets connected
song lines
created

sister poems
the word
became flesh

and loved
amongst us.

KOOKABURRA

The kookaburra, large
with wild flapping wings
came from behind
as I watched
the sun rising
over the mountain.

It was so big
my fear conjured
a dingo running
startled through the grass

Instead, it was
the rustling of wings
that took off high
into the arching branches
of a gum tree

It stared down at me
daring me to follow.

LEECH

I didn't feel the leech
I didn't feel
I didn't

I didn't sense
bloodsucking,
and pushed on
even though
the draining
left me vague
and dizzy

I didn't feel
I didn't

Small black worm
deep black magic
dark form
hidden

I didn't feel the leech
I didn't feel
I didn't

My eyes were
fixed on galaxies
staring at the
half-formed moon

I didn't feel the leech
I didn't feel
I didn't.

ABDITORY*

In the abditory
I place the precious bits of me

the ones I do not want to show
the ones I want no one to know

the salt of sea
the leaf of tree
the tiny cup of perfect tea
the memory of long ago
in the abditory

we're both free
naked just for us to see

the soul filled glow
the seeds to grow

you and me
in the abditory.

---

*A place for hiding things of value.
This poem was a writing prompt Joanne gave us at
Wind Spirit.

WIND SPIRIT

Ley line
song line
ley line lullaby

Invisible lines
connecting the land
across thousands of kilometres
and millions of years

Ley line
song line
ley line lullaby

Keepers of the earth,
birthers of her food,
she tends the
loamy soil

Ley line
song line
ley line lullaby

Hand in hand
as darkness falls
they guide
us to the spiral

Ley line
song line
ley line lullaby

Harmony of snakes
and sky,
water flows
and spirits high

Ley line
song line
ley line lullaby.

www.ingramcontent.com/pod-product-compliance
Lightning Source LLC
Chambersburg PA
CBHW011127070526
44584CB00028B/3812